KNIGHT SURVIVAL GUIDE

Anna Claybourne

Published 2011 by
A&C Black Publishers Ltd.
36 Soho Square, London, W1D 3QY

www.acblack.com

ISBN   HB 978-1-4081-3388-0
         PB 978-1-4081-3389-7

Text copyright © 2010 Anna Claybourne

This book is produced using paper that is made from wood grown in managed, sustainable forests. It is natural, renewable and recyclable. The logging and manufacturing processes conform to the environmental regulations of the country of origin.

Produced for A&C Black by Calcium. www.calciumcreative.co.uk

Printed and bound in China by C&C Offset Printing Co.

All the internet addresses given in this book were correct at the time of going to press. The author and publishers regret any inconvenience caused if addresses have changed or sites have ceased to exist, but can accept no responsibility for any such changes.

Acknowledgements

The publishers would like to thank the following for their kind permission to reproduce their photographs:

Cover: Shutterstock.
Pages: Corbis: Lebrecht Music & Arts 19; Dreamstime: Aleksander Lorenz 14, Thomas Ramage 1, 15; Shutterstock: Hintau Aliaksei 18, Bortel Pavel 20, CSLD 17, Demid 8, Dibrova 3, 12, Sergii Figurnyi 9, Abramova Kseniya 6, Steve Mann 13, Razumovskaya Marina Nikolaevna 7, PetrMalyshev 21, Nicholas Piccillo 4, Puchan 5, Raulin 10, St. Nick 11, Johannes Wiebel 16.

Contents

Tough Stuff

Being a knight is GREAT! You can fight in battles and go on big adventures – you even have your own horse!

Are you tough enough?

Being a knight is fun, but it's not an easy ride. You must be strong, tough, and very brave.

 Knights wear a lot of **armour**.

Armour

Heavy armour

A knight's armour was very heavy, so the horses they rode had to be super-strong.

A knight's job

Knights were soldiers who rode horses and went into battle for their king or **lord**.

Lord

In Training

You will start training to be a knight when you are seven years old. You will be sent to work in a lord's castle as a **page**.

A tough job

Life as a page is hard work. You must:

1 Take messages for your lord.
2 Learn good manners.
3 Tidy up after your lord and keep his rooms clean.

You will learn how to ride and fight.

Becoming a squire

At 14 years old, a page became a squire. Then he helped a knight with his horse and armour.

Squire

Into battle

Squires went into battle with their knight and fought by his side.

Fighting Talk

A knight's main job is to fight, so you will need top sword skills to beat your enemy. You will also need to train for battle.

Take that!

You will fight with a heavy sword. If you *can* lift it:

1 Swing it from side to side.
2 Use it to slash and bash!

Sticky head

If a knight hurt his head, his hair was shaved off, and his head was covered in oil, honey, and roses.

Pick a weapon

Knights used lots of weapons, including a **battle-axe**, **pike** or **lance**, and a **mace**.

Battle-axe

Hold your sword with two hands.

In Battle

You will need to be brave in battle. Charge straight in on horseback with your fellow knights and carry pikes to stab your **enemies**.

Cover up

Your enemies are soldiers with spears, bows, and arrows. To stay safe:

1   Wear armour.
2   Carry a shield.

No running away now!

Raining arrows

Knights fired rows of arrows at their enemies.

Hard head

Knights wore thick helmets to stop their heads and faces from being cut in battle.

Shield

Getting Caught

Knights' fights are dangerous and it is very hard to **survive**. Even if you do manage to stay alive, you might still be caught by your enemies.

Knight for sale

Your enemies will give you back to your lord – for a **ransom**. If your lord has enough cash (and if he likes you enough), you should be freed.

Pricey knights

To win back a really great knight, a lord would pay a ransom of lots of gold or land.

Fair fights

Captured knights were kept in a castle, but they were treated fairly.

Your lord will pay up if you are worth it!

Showing Off

When there are no real battles, take part in a **tournament**. This is a fighting competition in which you can show off your skills.

Charge!

To **joust** you must:

1 Ride towards your enemy at top speed.
2 Try to hit him with your lance.

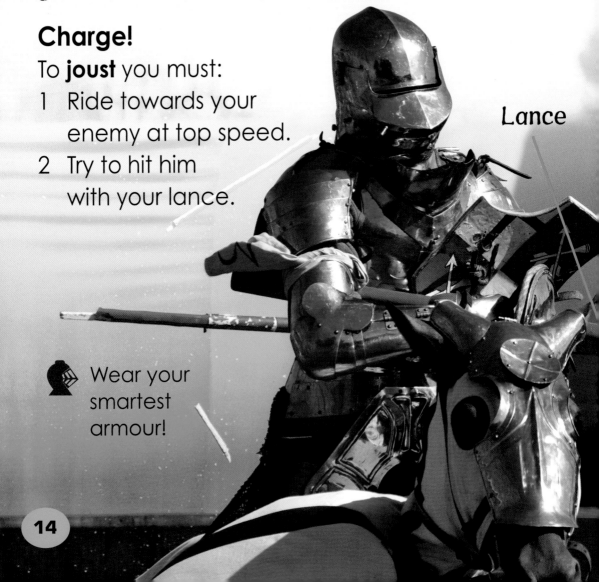

Lance

Wear your smartest armour!

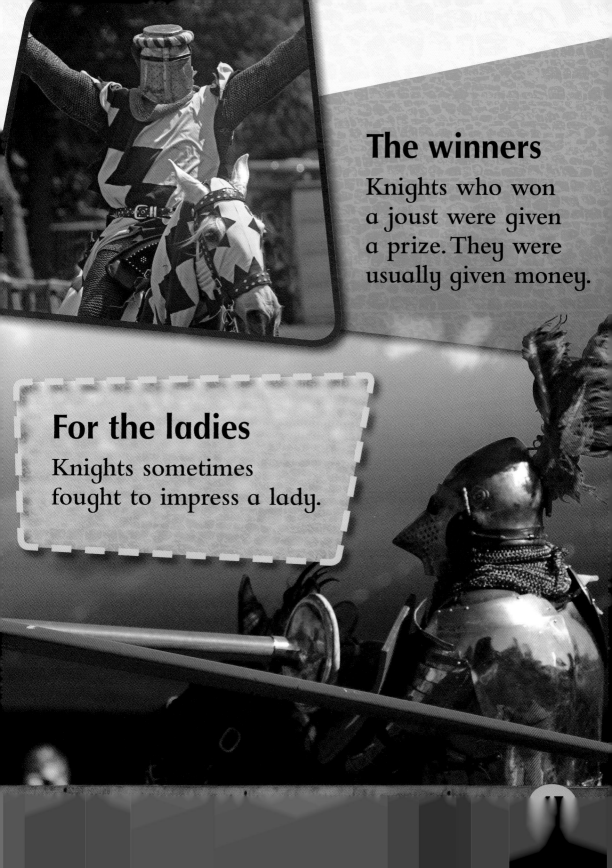

The winners

Knights who won a joust were given a prize. They were usually given money.

For the ladies

Knights sometimes fought to impress a lady.

Knight Rules

A good knight must be very polite to ladies. Always **bow** and kneel to a lady and never, ever swear at her!

Your special lady

You can even fight for a lady. In any fight, make sure you wear her family colours or **coat of arms**.

 Knights put their own coat of arms on their shields.

Take care

Knights were expected to **defend** and **protect** women.

Girls, too

Most knights were male but women could be knights, too. Joan of Arc was a girl and a famous French knight.

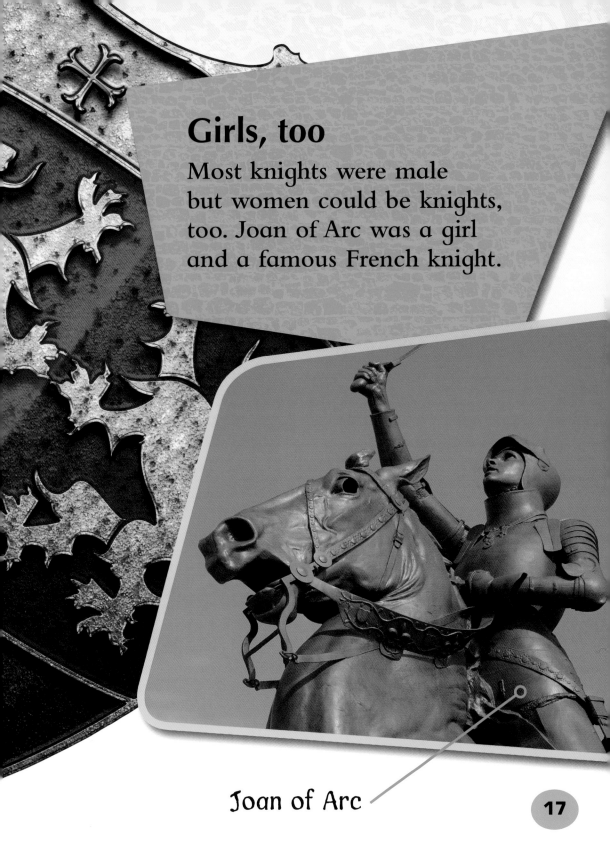

Joan of Arc

At Parties

As a knight, you will go to a lot of **feasts**. Talk to the ladies, play board games, and don't forget your manners.

It's my party!
If you have your own castle, you can throw feasts yourself. Use them to make friends with important people, such as kings.

Let's dance
Knights had to learn the latest dances to show off at parties.

Can you carve?

All knights were good at carving meat, and they showed off their carving at feasts.

Roast peacock is a favourite food at feasts.

On a Mission

Your king or lord might test you by sending you on a quest, or mission. You might have to catch an enemy or save a prisoner in a castle.

Top quests

If you are really lucky you might get to find treasure or rescue a princess from a tower. And all knights want to fight a dragon, of course!

Cup of magic

Some knights went on a great adventure to find a magical cup called the Holy Grail.

Famous knights

In many famous stories, knights rescued princesses or ladies who had been taken prisoner by a wicked lord or king.

Dragons are terrifying beasts!

Glossary

armour metal suit worn to protect the body in battle

battle-axe short, heavy axe

bow to bend over at the waist

coat of arms special family design

defend to stop something or someone from being hurt

enemies people who want to harm another person or other people

feasts parties where people eat lots of food

joust when two knights on horses charge at each other with lances

lance long, wooden pole

lord important man who had a large house or castle

mace long club with a heavy weight on the end

page boy training to be a knight

pike long-handled spear

protect to take care of something or someone

ransom money paid to set someone free

survive to stay alive

tournament contest where knights test their skills

Further Reading

Websites

Take a look at the knights activity village at:
**www.activityvillage.co.uk/knight_crafts_
and_costume.htm**

Try colouring in some knights at:
**www.kids-n-fun.com/coloringpages/kleurplaat_
Knights_88.aspx**

Try an online joust at:
www.tudorbritain.org/joust/index.asp

Books

*King Arthur and the Knights of the Round
Table* by Marcia Williams, Walker (2010).

Knight (Tough Jobs) by Helen Greathead,
A&C Black (2007).

Knights (Horrible Histories Handbooks)
by Terry Deary, Scholastic (2006).

Knights' Tales by Terry Deary, A&C Black (2009).

Index